1001 Things
Happy Couples
Know About
Marriage

Project Editor: Lisa Stilwell

Designed by ThinkPen Design, LLC

ISBN 978-1-4041-8751-1

Printed and bound in China

www.thomasnelson.com

09 10 11 12 (RRD) 5 4 3 2 1

1001 Things Happy Couples Know About Marriage

(Like Love, Romance, & Morning Breath)

HARRY H. HARRISON JR.

THOMAS NELSON
Since 1798

NASHVILLE   DALLAS   MEXICO CITY   RIO DE JANEIRO   BEIJING

Table of Contents

Preface

A *wedding* is a joyful celebration of two people being so in love they make a spiritual and public vow of their decision to come together. A *marriage* is what happens after the ceremony.

Weddings have become a huge money-making industry. But staying married is what couples really need to spend their time and energy on. It doesn't matter if you're getting married next week or if you've been married twenty-five years, you will face challenges and issues that could break you apart. This is why couples need to understand that marriage has less to do with maintaining that "new love" feeling than it has to do with commitment, kindness, forgiveness, and, quite possibly, a mother-in-law.

The fact is, being married is the only thing you can do for fifty years and still not be good at. Indeed many people are better at marriage in the beginning than they are at the end. So what's the secret? Well, the secret is, there is no "the" secret. But there are some 1001 things you need to know about marriage that can help determine your level of happiness and success.

That's what makes this book so necessary. It's not just about staying in love. It's about something much more important . . . . It's about staying married.

Marriage Plans

1. You need to know the marriage
is more important than the wedding.
And requires even more planning.

●

2. You need to know your
relationship will be sanctified.

●

3. You need to know you're
promising "till death do you part."
Not "till the good times end."

●

4. You need to know to marry for
character more than for good looks
or money. Okay, a *little* more.

●

5. You need to know to use
your mind as well as your heart
when you choose a spouse.

6. You need to know a happy
couple is made up of two individuals
committed to each other.

•

7. You need to know about
Trash to Treasure, where you can find
everything from wedding gowns used once
to deep-discount wedding decorations.
Go to TheNest.com, then click on
Community, then Trash to Treasure.

•

8. You need to know you're choosing
the person you'll spend the rest
of your life with. And still make
passes at when you're both on walkers.

9. You need to know you're
launching into a fifty-year
conversation, interrupted by life.

•

10. You need to know it's normal to think
this whole wedding thing is a mistake.

•

11. You need to know that
a happy marriage is the art
of putting the other person first.

•

12. You need to know a $100,000
wedding can be a down payment
on a fantastic home. Think about it.

13. You need to know to
not put off marriage because
you can't afford the wedding.
You can get married for fifty bucks.

•

14. You need to know if you
start with a budget instead of the
guest list, you can maintain control
over your wedding expenses.

•

15. You need to know the last thing you
want to do is get in hock over your
wedding. Scale back grandiose plans.

16. You need to know to register your wedding at practical stores like Target and Crate and Barrel, not just the fantasy stores like Neiman Marcus and Tiffany's. You need pots to cook in.

•

17. You need to know to delete your old flames from your cell phone. Inviting them to the wedding is a dumb idea too.

•

18. You need to know to define for yourselves what *husband* and *wife* mean. Don't rely on some book.

19. You need to know nature never intended for you to maintain that overwhelming feeling of new love forever. To begin with, your brain would probably explode.

●

20. You need to know that scientists have found there's totally different brain chemistry at work in couples who've been in long-term marriages from in newly-in-love couples.

●

21. You need to know that marrying, raising children, and sending them out into society makes a huge impact on your community and the world.

22. You need to know things change the moment you say, "I do." Don't think your life together will be like it was when you were dating.

•

23. You need to know to not expect lifelong bliss, free of problems, quarrels, or issues. You will be disappointed. Guaranteed.

•

24. You need to know from the beginning that love is a decision. Sometimes you make that decision after a fight. Or when temptation walks in the door.

•

25. You need to know your husband or wife cannot be your complete source of happiness. You'll still need friends. Family. And a hobby. Men will need a TV.

26. You need to know that just because you're married, the two of you won't do everything together. In fact, it's important you don't do everything together.

•

27. You need to know you have to be able to live without each other. This way you can love each other without feeling like you own each other.

•

28. You need to know one of the best wedding gifts you can get for yourselves is a marriage skills training weekend.

29. You need to know you can't let yourself go to pot after you get married. There are a number of benefits to exercising and eating right that have nothing to do with health.

•

30. You need to know to talk about your plans and dreams with each other.

•

31. You need to know to be on the same page about having babies. When you want one. When your spouse wants one. And does one of you not want to stop until you have seven.

•

32. You need to know you should always tell each other the truth. Unless she asks you if you think she looks fat.

33. You need to know to help each other chase your personal dreams. It could be writing a book, going back to college, or starting a company. Be each other's cheerleader.

•

34. You need to know to pray together. Start now.

•

35. You need to know to never criticize each other in public. This can have far-reaching consequences.

•

36. You need to know that if you can successfully share one bathroom, one sink, one tub, and one shower, the odds are good you'll stay married.

37. You need to know to take care of yourself. One of your primary jobs as a husband or wife is to stay around.

•

38. You need to know you're not marrying a fantasy, but a flesh-and-blood person with their own dreams and expectations—and annoying habits and strange idiosyncrasies.

•

39. You need to know each other's health histories. Does anyone have herpes? Diabetes? A fondness for vodka? Love each other enough to reveal what you're both getting into.

40. You need to know if your future spouse's family has a history of mental illness. That kind of history can impact generations.

●

41. You need to know to travel all you can while you're young. When you're older, there will be kids, financial pressure, and let's face it, a lingering desire to catch up on your sleep.

●

42. You need to know that a simple stroll in the park can be romantic. Especially if you leave your cell phones at home.

●

43. You need to know that regular family mealtime is important. Guard it.

44. You need to know the other person will always love your compliments.

•

45. You need to know to show respect at all times. Even if you're furious with each other. Respect keeps fights from escalating.

•

46. You need to know how to make each other feel adored.

•

47. You need to know everybody has a past. Be gentle with it.

•

48. You need to know your actions say as much about your feelings as your words do. But it's still important to say the words.

49. You need to know married couples find life less stressful than unmarried couples who live together.

•

50. You need to know a person won't change just because you marry them. If she's a gambler before you get married, she'll be a gambler after you get married. Only now she has your money to cover her losses.

•

51. You need to know one of you must manage the money. Someone must pay the bills, keep the family on budget, and be the bad guy when tough decisions need to be made. And the other needs to respect those decisions.

52. You need to know happy couples laugh together a lot. If you don't have a sense of humor, seriously consider developing one.

•

53. You need to know there are some things she might not give up, even for the sake of the marriage. Like sleeping with the heat on in the summer.

•

54. You need to know what couples fight about: money, sex, how many children to have, where to worship, even *if* to worship, and what to eat.

55. You need to know to celebrate each other's successes, no matter how small. You'll be amazed at how successful each of you becomes.

•

56. You need to know if you first graduate from college, then marry, then have children, the odds of your marriage succeeding are good.

•

57. You need to know that saying "I do" means you get to grow old with your best friend.

•

58. You need to know to say, "I love you" three or four times a day even when what you really want to say is, "Why is this MasterCard bill so high?"

59. You need to know to make major decisions together. Don't buy a car or lease an apartment as a surprise. It will be.

•

60. You need to know the other person has to get their way some of the time. It will feel like most of the time. They're thinking the same thing.

•

61. You need to know a little kindness will help smooth a lot of the bumpy spots.

•

62. You need to know you can be happy even when the other person isn't. It's a trait found in solid marriages.

63. You need to know you're going to have to compromise on the thermostat.

•

64. You need to know not all your dreams will be shared. Like your dream about backpacking through the Amazon. It may be yours alone.

•

65. You need to know any electric blanket you put on the bed must have dual controls.

•

66. You need to know you can no longer have best friends of the opposite sex.

67. You need to know a marriage isn't a place to keep secrets. Like your secret love for sitar music. He's going to find out.

•

68. You need to know your spouse should be the most important person in your life.

•

69. You need to know the flavor of the wedding cake or the color of the bridesmaids' dresses doesn't impact the quality of the marriage. At all.

•

70. You need to know to establish a routine. Don't be scared of that word. Routine is a good thing.

71. You need to know to practice the fine art of not saying the first thing that pops into your brain.

•

72. You need to know the strongest marriages are made up of two independent people who love each other, not two needy people who are dependent upon each other.

•

73. You need to know an ideal family can be found anywhere love grows and flourishes.

•

74. You need to know to talk about each other's day, every day, even though she just wants to take a bath and he just wants to watch *24*.

75. You need to know to try and
look good at home. Don't just put on
stretch shorts and a Grateful Dead T-shirt
and assume you look fetching.

•

76. You need to know to be constantly
aware of the health of your marriage. Does
it need attention? A vacation? A babysitter?

•

77. You need to know happy couples tend
to go along with each other's wishes.
Except maybe to the tractor pull.
Or the scrapbooking store.
Then you're on your own.

78. You need to know a happy marriage means finding the one person in the world who accepts you as you are. Well, if you'd just shave. And not use your sleeve as a Kleenex. And pick up your shoes.

•

79. You need to know that if you can't talk about money and sex, your marriage will never make it.

•

80. You need to know how to express heated emotion without cursing, yelling, making accusations, or throwing things. Even though they were all effective when you were a teenager.

81. You need to know the best way
to change your wife's attitude
is to change your own.

•

82. You need to know you might have to
learn to sleep with someone who makes
noises at night. Strange noises.

•

83. You need to know that, in the
beginning, you'll desire each other
more than a good night's sleep.

•

84. You need to know this won't always
be true. But that doesn't mean you're
falling out of love. You just need sleep.

85. You need to know it's important you both believe the other will stand by you.

•

86. You need to know to thank God for every anniversary. And to go all out on the big ones.

•

87. You need to know to take pictures of each other from day one. Years later, they'll remind you of what a hot number you married.

•

88. You need to know that whatever you look for in each other, you'll find.

•

89. You need to know there's not a marriage problem that love, compassion, forgiveness, and respect can't solve.

90. You need to know, as life gets more complicated, your marriage might too.

•

91. You need to know marriage means it's time to quit hanging out with your single friends.

•

92. You need to know to make friends and hang out with happily married couples. These relationships increase the likelihood of you staying together.

•

93. You need to know that sometimes you need to talk to your best girlfriend more than you need to talk to your husband.

94. You need to know that a loving
marriage is like a living thing.
You have to nourish it daily.

•

95. You need to know each of you
will have your own opinions, beliefs,
interests, and faults. Take, for instance,
World Extreme Cagefighting. Incredibly,
she might not see the value of it.

•

96. You need to know to not make fun
of each other. The other person
will never see the humor.

97. You need to know to change your
MySpace and Facebook pages
to "Couple" status. So everyone
will know you are now a "we."

•

98. You need to know that if your parents
divorced, it's natural to worry that
disaster will strike your marriage too.

•

99. You need to know that even if your
parents divorced several times, that isn't a
predictor of your marriage. Your thoughts
and actions are more important factors.

Marriage and Love

100. You need to know there'll be some days you'll have to really work at loving the other person. Especially those days when she's snarling at you.

•

101. You need to know that love is showing patience for a man who hasn't picked up his laundry in three days.

•

102. You need to know love is caring more about another person's happiness than your own.

103. You need to know true love is loving another person in spite of their annoying little habits that would drive another person nuts.

●

104. You need to know love is letting another person lean on you.

●

105. You need to know love is listening.

●

106. You need to know love is reassuring your pregnant wife that her gas problems don't embarrass you.

107. You need to know that love is agreeing to go to a therapist even though you think it's the other person who has a few loose screws.

•

108. You need to know love is what God says it is: patient, kind, truthful, not envious, not self-seeking.

•

109. You need to know that on some days you will love your spouse more than you do on other days. It doesn't mean your relationship has hit the skids. More than anything, it just means you need to hold each other for a while.

110. You need to know love
is accepting that you're not
always going to get your way.

•

111. You need to know
love doesn't give orders.

•

112. You need to know love
is accepting her hormones.

•

113. You need to know love is getting
hugged even though you're contagious
and snot is dripping out of your nose.

114. You need to know love is letting you fall asleep on his shoulder even though he had rotator cuff surgery three days ago.

•

115. You need to know love is understanding how hard the other one is trying.

•

116. You need to know jealousy isn't a sign of love. It's a sign of being a loon.

•

117. You need to know love is what remains after the infatuation ends.

•

118. You need to know love isn't a feeling word. It's an action word.

119. You need to know love will not take care of everything. You also need money, prayer, determination, and a big screen.

●

120. You need to know that sexual fidelity, kindness, generosity, and cooperation are surefire ways to maintain love in a relationship.

●

121. You need to know being loved means someone else cares as much about you as you do.

●

122. You need to know people who love each other treasure spending time with each other.

123. You need to know love is showing him you respect him. Even if he's lost his job, money's tight, and your sister just moved into a brand new house.

•

124. You need to know love is planting a soft, romantic kiss on her cheek while she's washing the dishes. And then telling her to sit down while you finish.

•

125. You need to know love is reminding him of his successes and accomplishments when he feels like a failure.

126. You need to know love is eating
whatever has been cooked for dinner.
Even if it's artichoke hearts. Or grilled
lamb patties. And remember
this line: "This tastes great."

•

127. You need to know that no matter how
hard you try not to, you will
hurt each other. But it helps to try.

•

128. You need to know that,
at the end of the day, commitment
is more important than love.

Marriage and Faith

129. You need to know God
has brought you together.

•

130. You need to know you've made
a covenant with your spouse.
Not a business contract.

•

131. You need to know to turn your
marriage over to God every morning.
He has some thoughts about it.

•

132. You need to know to agree
beforehand what role faith will
play in your marriage. And what
role it will play when things go south.

133. You need to know that you must be
at peace with God before you
can be at peace in your marriage.

•

134. You need to know that if
you make your spouse your god,
they will always disappoint you.

•

135. You need to know to not try
to change your spouse's beliefs.
That's God's job. Not yours.

•

136. You need to know a spiritual
foundation is vital to a healthy marriage.
There will be times when it carries you.

137. You need to know that
marriage isn't about the two of you.
It's about the three of you.

•

138. You need to know not everyone draws
close to God in the same way. You and your
spouse may be on different paths.
Perhaps even on different planets.

•

139. You need to know that if
you make your spouse the source
of all your happiness, you've
limited what God can do for you.

140. You need to know that instead of arguing with your spouse about going to church, ask him or her to pray with you about something: your finances, your children, your health. Take baby steps.

•

141. You need to know you can pray to become a better husband or wife. God pays attention to those prayers.

•

142. You need to know that saying grace at mealtime is one way to start praying together.

143. You need to know that sometimes having a strong faith in God can cause a fight. Evidence we live in a fallen world. And a great time to practice forgiveness, patience, and faith.

•

144. You need to know that prayer brings divine power into your relationship.

•

145. You need to know that giving back to God somehow strengthens your marriage.

•

146. You need to know to talk to each other about your beliefs. You don't have to agree. You do have to talk.

147. You need to know that when you focus on the wonderful things about your partner, God can focus on providing for your needs.

•

148. You need to know that praying to God to change your spouse is telling God what to do.

•

149. You need to know to find a place of worship that you can support wholeheartedly and attend regularly. If your spouse comes, even better.

•

150. You need to know a strong marriage means someone is praying for you every night.

151. You need to know you can spice up your marriage with a spiritual retreat. And you thought you needed Vegas.

•

152. You need to know the only way to change a person is to start praising them. This is really hard when you see credit card bills piling up and laundry lying on the floor, but it works.

•

153. You need to know both optimism and pessimism work as intended on a marriage.

•

154. You need to know to be gentle.

155. You need to know to admit when you're wrong. Single people can't do this.

•

156. You need to know to thank God daily for the love you've found in each other.

•

157. You need to know to find a place to worship when you're on vacation. Don't leave your spirituality at home.

•

158. You need to know that rock-solid marriages aren't built on watching TV every night, but on daily discussions that begin with "Tell me about your day."

159. You need to know forgiveness isn't a sign of weakness. Resentments are.

•

160. You need to know to agree beforehand if your baby boy will be baptized or circumcised. Or both.

•

161. You need to know God didn't call us to love one another only when the other person is lovable.

•

162. You need to know to not get in the way of your spouse's relationship with God.

163. You need to know friends, family, faith, and traditions can strengthen a marriage. Or shake it up.

•

164. You need to know that teaching a Sunday school class or leading a youth group together is a good way to learn about kids before you have them.

•

165. You need to know to keep a place inside you reserved for God alone.

Marriage Myths

166. You need to know having a stress-free life together is a myth. What you will have is someone to face the stress with.

167. You need to know it's a myth that marriage changes people. But people can change a marriage.

168. You need to know a perfect marriage requires perfect people. Which is a myth.

169. You need to know it's a myth that a happy couple agrees about everything. In fact, some of the happiest couples may rarely agree about anything. Except to love and accept each other.

170. You need to know that never going to bed angry is a myth. If couples never went to bed angry, they would be sleep deprived.

•

171. You need to know it's a myth that marriage will make you happier. If you're unhappy now, you'll be just as unhappy later.

•

172. You need to know that living happily ever after is a myth. There'll be days where you'd be happier living in Siberia as a goat herder.

•

173. You need to know it's a myth to think you'll be joyously in love every day.

174. You need to know it's a myth that you'll be on the same spiritual plane. Everybody has a uniquely personal relationship with God that changes throughout life.

•

175. You need to know that being happy in an "open marriage" is a myth. Adultery weighs on your soul.

•

176. You need to know that thinking you'll do everything together is a myth. Doing what you don't want to do over and over again will just make you unhappy.

•

177. You need to know it's a myth that she'll complete you. That's a movie line.

178. You need to know it's a myth that having a baby will bring you closer. If you don't work at it, a baby will drive you apart.

•

179. You need to know it's a myth that romantic love is the basis for long-term marriages. Romantic love ends in about a year.

•

180. You need to know it's a myth that sex won't matter as you get older. The reality is sex gets better.

•

181. You need to know your every dream won't be fulfilled by marriage. But miracles you haven't even imagined will happen.

Marriage and Happiness

182. You need to know studies indicate a good marriage makes you as happy as putting $100,000 a year into your savings account. This doesn't mean that getting married ten times will make you feel like a millionaire.

•

183. You need to know marriage improves your sex life. That should make you happy.

•

184. You need to know marriage keeps people alive longer. Scientists don't know why.

•

185. You need to know one key to marriage happiness is not to tell the other person every time he does something wrong. Breathe deep. Don't open your mouth.

186. You need to know marriage reduces
stress and stress-related illnesses.
In other words, you may be mad at your
spouse, but it's better than being
mad at life. With no one to snap at.

●

187. You need to know love and praise
are contagious. The more love and praise
you offer, the more of it you get back.

●

188. You need to know that a willingness
to sacrifice your needs for your partner
is directly linked to a happy marriage.

●

189. You need to know happy
couples have sex more often.

190. You need to know people who abandon bad marriages have a hard time for a couple of years, but often wind up happier than they were before.

●

191. You need to know that married people who have sex outside of marriage are not as happy as married people who don't.

●

192. You need to know that scientists agree that married people are less nuts. Research shows they suffer less psychological stress than single adults do.

193. You need to know people who are unhappy before they get married tend to be unhappy in their marriage.

•

194. You need to know one reason God puts us in a marriage is so we can find joy in serving someone other than ourselves.

•

195. You need to know marriage means there's somebody around to take care of you when you're sick or depressed. That is enough to make anyone happy.

196. You need to know fear is marriage's greatest enemy. And gratitude is its greatest building block. Doctors say that your brain can't feel both at the same time.

•

197. You need to know your thoughts can make you happy. You can actually increase your marital happiness by focusing your thoughts several times a day on something you treasure: your spouse's humor, your home, or even music you like.

•

198. You need to know people grow fond of people who make them laugh.

199. You need to know men who marry are less likely to be arrested. They're busy doing chores. And that makes wives happy.

•

200. You need to know married adults drink less than single adults. One theory is they don't spend all night in a bar trying to pick somebody up.

•

201. You need to know that extreme hardship early in marriage doesn't have to be a deal breaker. In fact, it can virtually cement a relationship.

202. You need to know one key
to curing an unhappy marriage is
one of you deciding to be happier.

•

203. You need to know that whatever you
look for in your spouse, you'll tend to find.

•

204. You need to know researchers have
found that having money and a strong
marriage are keys to personal happiness.

205. You need to know if your spouse is happy, you're more likely to recover from surgery faster.

•

206. You need to know married adults who make above $30,000 are just as likely to say they're very happy as rich, single, unmarried adults.

•

207. You need to know the best predictor of individual happiness is a loving relationship and the amount of time we invest in it.

Marriage and Sex

208. You need to know men and women think differently about sex. To begin with, he's usually thinking about it.

•

209. You need to know to invite God into the bedroom. Hey, the whole thing is His idea.

•

210. You need to know sex between a husband and wife is sacred.

•

211. You need to know sex was created by God as a gift for married couples.

•

212. You need to know you were designed to desire your spouse.

213. You need to know that in a loving marriage, sex is like icing on the cake. The cake, however, is made up of love and faith and kindness and patience and respect.

•

214. You need to know if sex stops in a marriage, the marriage itself is not far behind.

•

215. You need to know giving your body to your spouse is a spiritual act. An offering of yourself.

•

216. You need to know how to talk about sex without ego, emotion, or embarrassment.

217. You need to know it's easy to give your body to your spouse in your 20s when you look great. But it's just as important to do so in your 60s, even when you're not sure how you measure up.

•

218. You need to know to agree on what the bedroom is for. Is it a place to watch TV or a place to make love and go to sleep?

•

219. You need to know good sex includes the talking and laughing afterward. Don't just roll over and pass out.

220. You need to know the odds are overwhelming that you'll have some sexual problems at some point in your relationship. But there's nothing that can't be worked through.

•

221. You need to know you can choose to be a generous, enthusiastic, kind lover or a selfish, reluctant, demanding one. Guess who has the happier marriage?

•

222. You need to know being able to talk about sex is as important as actually doing it.

•

223. You need to know criticism is not an aphrodisiac.

224. You need to know greater intimacy leads to better sex.

•

225. You need to know that scheduling sex is a good way to end struggles over it. If everyone knows it's Tuesday and Saturday, the person with the lower sex drive isn't always saying "no" and the partner with the higher sex drive isn't always getting shot down. Romance ensues.

•

226. You need to know no one is born a good lover. We have to be taught. By our spouse.

•

227. You need to know if there's a problem in your sex life, there's usually a problem somewhere else.

228. You need to know married
couples have better sex lives than couples
who aren't married. Except for single
people on TV and in the movies.

•

229. You need to know even
the best marriages have roadblocks
to good sex. Like teenagers.

•

230. You need to know the woman who
wants satin lingerie in her twenties will
want cotton flannel pj's in her forties. And
will wear a sweater coat to bed in her fifties.

•

231. You need to know passion
for your spouse can light up
passion for all kinds of things in life.

232. You need to know to make sex a form of prayer. You're thanking God for the gift of your spouse and their love for you.

•

233. You need to know an exciting, fulfilling sex life means being willing to try new things as well as sacrificing your needs to your partner's.

•

234. You need to know to show each other affection throughout the day. Not just in the bedroom in the evening.

•

235. You need to know that if you wait until you're in the mood, the other person could be asleep.

236. You need to know that if a two-year-old has been throwing up on her, she's been sitting in the carpool lane for an hour without air conditioning, she rushed to put dinner on the table, and she just had a fight with her mom . . . this might be a bad time to try and get something started.

237. You need to know your spouse might really have a headache.

238. You need to know the only thing kids will do for your love life is ruin it. It's God's way of holding down the population.

239. You need to know to start earlier as you get older. Even the most passionate couples are generally passed out by 10:30 p.m.

•

240. You need to know if you're a kind and considerate lover, you don't have to worry about your performance.

•

241. You need to know your spouse's likes and fears. Nobody needs to be surprised in the bedroom.

242. You need to know that, contrary to popular myth, sex gets better the longer you're married. (Fifty years from now you could shock your grandkids.)

•

243. You need to know that if you don't hold and touch and show affection throughout the day, your sex life will be miserable.

Marriage Problems

244. You need to know to discuss difficult issues before you get married, not when you're on the way out the door.

•

245. You need to know that the honeymoon feeling of love—you know, when everything is new and wonderful and exciting—can end before the wedding. And this has nothing to do with whether or not you'll be happy as a couple.

•

246. You need to know the first two years of marriage carry the highest risk of affairs and divorce.

247. You need to know that if
you think your spouse has changed,
look at yourself. Maybe you no
longer find his drinking amusing.

•

248. You need to know marriage
is no place for rugged individualism.

•

249. You need to know women
tend to start more conversations about
problems in the relationship than
men do. Men are happy if they're
holding the remote control.

250. You need to know problems are part of life. Divorce doesn't have to be.

•

251. You need to know if you're having trouble sleeping together, a bigger bed might solve everything.

•

252. You need to know if you're unhappy, you're also to blame.

•

253. You need to know to work on yourself. It's more productive than trying to change the other person.

254. You need to know if you focus more on your golf game than on your marriage, you will wind up shooting in the high 70s. And enjoying the single life.

•

255. You need to know a couple's joy is based on the ability of the husband and wife to adjust to things beyond their control.

•

256. You need to know if you worry all the time, you could be slowly killing your marriage.

•

257. You need to know to not say everything that enters your mind.

258. You need to know criticism ("You never," "You should," "You always,") slowly corrodes a marriage.

•

259. You need to know your spouse can sense when something is wrong. If you've had a bad day or you're coming down with a migraine, say so. Don't let them think you're angry.

•

260. You need to know that if you let yourself get to the point where you start feeling contempt for your partner, you'll forget why you fell in love with them.

261. You need to know that denying all responsibility for the problems you're facing is a problem.

•

262. You need to know it's easier to see the defensiveness in your partner than in yourself.

•

263. You need to know that constantly complaining about your marriage to anyone who'll listen will lead to you having no one to complain about.

•

264. You need to know blame doesn't make a marriage stronger.

265. You need to know that when you make accusations about what your partner is thinking ("You think I don't know what I'm doing"), you're setting the stage for a no-win argument.

•

266. You need to know that if you respond to your partner's complaint with a bigger complaint of your own and totally ignore what's been said, you're avoiding responsibility. And the fight will go on.

•

267. You need to know if you're still mad about something that happened five years ago, it's a sign you're off your meds.

268. You need to know the less defensive you act during an argument, the sooner your partner will realize you're actually listening to what they're saying.

•

269. You need to know that stonewalling—responding to a complaint or criticism with the silent treatment—tells your spouse you really don't care much about the marriage.

•

270. You need to know not talking about a problem often leads to bigger problems.

•

271. You need to know if you bring your anger from work into the house, you'll now have problems in both places.

272. You need to know to be on time. Be on time for dinner, be on time when you meet somewhere. Don't keep the other one hanging. It causes problems.

•

273. You need to know if you put up with lying, drugs, alcohol, or infidelity early in your marriage, the later years will only be worse.

•

274. You need to know a lack of food, energy, sleep, or exercise can cause even the most mild-mannered person to lose it over a dirty dish.

275. You need to know to fight
the urge to scold, nag, and whine.
Sometimes it's a battle.

•

276. You need to know that when someone
is suffering from depression, you can't
cheer them up. Men doing the dishes won't
even help. A doctor is what's needed.

•

277. You need to know if you're spending
all your time blogging online about the
state of your marriage instead of actually
talking to your husband, you have an issue.

278. You need to know if you are watching TV for three hours a night but spending only ten minutes in conversation, you have an issue.

●

279. You need to know if you don't want to have any more sex with your spouse, you have an issue.

●

280. You need to know if you find yourselves screaming at each other over whether to have squash or spinach for dinner, you have other problems.

281. You need to know that if you focus on each other's imperfections, they will only grow larger in your mind.

•

282. You need to know if you have to tell your spouse, "You can't take a joke," you probably didn't tell one.

•

283. You need to know to let go of your compulsion to control your spouse. You're not helping; you're actually driving them crazy.

•

284. You need to know moving can cause problems. Moving to a new city can be marriage altering.

285. You need to know that if you can't
give up alcohol or drugs for
your marriage, you have issues.

•

286. You need to know you're entitled to a
life of sobriety and sanity. So are your kids.

•

287. You need to know if your friends think
your marriage has issues, you have issues.

•

288. You need to know if you have low
self-esteem, you'll think your
wife feels the same way about you.

289. You need to know that
blaming your spouse makes you
sound like an eight-year-old.

•

290. You need to know that when people
feel powerless, they get scared.

•

291. You need to know if you can't control
your spending, you'll have issues.

•

292. You need to know if you're always
taking money out of savings to cover your
spending, you have issues.

293. You need to know if you're always taking a pill to ease the stress, you have issues.

•

294. You need to know if you fight with each other every time you drink, you have issues.

•

295. You need to know if you can't stop criticizing your spouse, you have issues.

•

296. You need to know if you're a moody person, you're hard to live with.

•

297. You need to know a solid marriage is built on cooperation. Not control.

298. You need to know working late
all the time can lead to issues.

•

299. You need to know a crazy
mother-in-law can be an issue.
Two crazy mothers-in-law can
be reason to move overseas.

•

300. You need to know that
if your spouse is afraid of you
or your reactions, you have issues.

•

301. You need to know that if
he's into porn, you have issues.

•

302. You need to know if someone isn't
getting enough sleep, you will have issues.

303. You need to know if you attack each other's self-esteem, you have issues.

•

304. You need to know if you come home from work tired, hungry, and angry, chances are really good you're primed for a fight. With the nearest available target.

•

305. You need to know if you constantly criticize yourself, you'll be prone to constantly criticize your wife.

•

306. You need to know that living together before you get engaged increases the likelihood you'll marry a loser for no other reason than he's there and you know he's available. Now you have real problems.

307. You need to know if you can't be alone with each other—if you constantly need people around you—you have issues.

•

308. You need to know there is a point of no return if you wait too long to deal with problems.

•

309. You need to know these nine words that can change a relationship: "I was wrong. I am sorry. Please forgive me."

Marriage Fights

310. You need to know that when you're married, there's a lot more to disagree about than when you were just dating.

•

311. You need to know expressing anger and disagreement in a positive way can make a marriage stronger.

•

312. You need to know the quickest way to start a fight is to start comparing each other to other people.

•

313. You need to know to not throw around the "D" word. Used often enough, everyone could start believing it's a possibility.

314. You need to know marital discord is one of the leading causes of human suffering.

•

315. You need to know fighting with each other can make you nuts. Relationship difficulties are one of the most common reasons people seek psychological services.

•

316. You need to know that instead of trying to win an argument, the best thing to do is let everyone cool off. Put it on hold a few hours or days. See if the issue is still there when you come back.

317. You need to know to calm yourself down during marriage storms. (Not easy, but possible.) Science has shown that once heart rates soar, rationality leaves the room.

•

318. You need to know to learn to slow down your breathing during arguments. You're less likely to say something stupid.

•

319. You need to know if you think your husband can solve all your problems, you're going to have problems.

•

320. You need to know women argue differently from men. She'll threaten to leave; he'll want to watch TV.

321. You need to know that even if you get a divorce, odds are you'll marry the same kind of person all over again. And have the same kinds of fights.

•

322. You need to know what your spouse thinks you're saying. Have him repeat your words. What he's heard will amaze you.

•

323. You need to know research has shown that happily married couples use certain words and actions to keep arguments from spiraling out of control. Phrases like "Please let me finish," "That hurt my feelings," and "Yes, I see" have a way of keeping the discussion constructive, bringing it to a conclusion faster, and still being friends afterward.

324. You need to know that instead of just criticizing your partner during a conflict, also say what you love about them. It changes the tone.

•

325. You need to know if you learn to listen without reacting defensively, you'll slow your partner's attack, and they'll drop their defenses.

•

326. You need to know that thousands of years of research indicate most people respond to anger with . . . well . . . anger.

•

327. You need to know that no matter how soft you think you talk during a fight, the other person will think you are yelling.

328. You need to know arguing about the past is an indication of a lack of forgiveness in your marriage.

•

329. You need to know you're a fallen human being too.

•

330. You need to know happy couples fight. But they always fight for their relationship.

•

331. You need to know to respect your partner's privacy. Reading his private notes, diaries, and journals will only shock you, start a fight, and damage your relationship.

332. You need to know a perfectly rational act during the middle of a fight is to leave the scene, go outside, and ask God what He was thinking when He made the opposite sex. Maybe He'll share.

•

333. You need to know that if your fighting is beginning to define your marriage, it's time to go to a Bible study.

•

334. You need to know patience has never started a fight.

•

335. You need to know people tend not to listen to people who are attacking them.

•

336. You need to know bringing up ancient history has never ended a fight.

337. You need to know
sarcasm dissolves love.

•

338. You need to know, before a fight
escalates into World War III, to ask
yourself, "How important is this?"
If it's not that important, move
on and get dinner on the table.

•

339. You need to know that instead of
explaining your side once again, you
need to listen to their perspective.

•

340. You need to know you must
fight fair. Telling her she's as
crazy as her mother—not fair.

341. You need to know listening can help you avoid a lot of fights. Like when he says, "I think we're spending too much money," he's not accusing you of being like your mother.

•

342. You need to know if you think it's your fault, it probably is.

•

343. You need to know that coming home tired, angry, hungry, and on edge is a good indicator of how the night will go if you're not careful.

•

344. You need to know that truly hurtful comments are off limits.

345. You need to know
to never fight by e-mail.

•

346. You need to know marriage
doesn't give you permission to
fight harder and scream louder.
In fact, marriage is an invitation to
always deal with your spouse lovingly.

•

347. You need to know if you don't say
anything mean and cruel, you'll have
one less thing to apologize for.

•

348. You need to know to not take literally
most things said in the heat of battle.

349. You need to know when you've been
acting like an idiot—and stop.

•

350. You need to know not every
conflict needs to be fought.

•

351. You need to know to show contrition.
Sometimes even when you're not
sure why the other person is angry.

•

352. You need to know that being married
requires you to be adult enough to
admit when a fight is your fault.

353. You need to know showing
humility and compassion ends more
fights than yelling and accusing.

•

354. You need to know making
an apology, even when you're
not in the wrong, is sometimes
required to restore sanity and peace.

•

355. You need to know that going
home to your parents is not an option.
You are home. Work it out.

356. You need to know you're biologically wired to remain physically agitated after an argument. This is a good time to ask God to shut your mouth.

•

357. You need to know that the more skills you have at defusing arguments, the happier you'll be.

•

358. You need to know to not let little things build up into a big thing.

•

359. You need to know a soft answer really does turn away wrath.

360. You need to know loving people can do hurtful things. This includes you.

•

361. You need to know to distinguish between your spouse and their actions. Love one; address the other.

•

362. You need to know that listening doesn't mean just waiting for the other person to stop talking so you can start.

•

363. You need to know that if you pray together before you begin discussing an issue, things are less likely to escalate out of control.

Marriage and
Forgiveness

382. You need to know a marriage can survive garlic breath, snoring, financial collapse, perhaps even infidelity. But it can't survive without forgiveness.

•

383. You need to know marriage isn't built on how you handle the easy moments, but how you get through the difficult ones.

•

384. You need to know you'll find it easier to forgive a serial killer than your wife for saying something hurtful.

•

385. You need to know silence, moodiness, and sulking are evidence you're holding on to the problem.

386. You need to know you don't have to wait until the other person apologizes first. Just say, "I'm sorry."

•

387. You need to know that forgiveness and peacemaking and problem solving are three of your primary responsibilities. And three keys to a successful marriage.

•

388. You need to know you can work to forgive someone right after a fight, or you can wait twenty-four hours to sulk about it and get steamed all over again.

•

389. You need to know forgiving someone isn't going to necessarily make that person change. But it will change you.

390. You need to know
to not take personally your
partner's inconsideration.

•

391. You need to know marriage
is not always 50/50.

•

392. You need to know that those
cute little quirks of his that caused
you to fall in love with him may set
your teeth on edge five years later.

•

393. You need to know forgiving your
partner can lead to lower blood pressure,
a lower heart rate, less depression,
and more fun on Friday night.

394. You need to know forgiveness
of your spouse is key to having
your own faults forgiven. Look it up.

•

395. You need to know to ask God
to help you see the problem
through your spouse's eyes.

•

396. You need to know sometimes you're
going to have to forgive your spouse
even though he hasn't asked for it.

•

397. You need to know forgiveness
doesn't excuse the other person's
words or behavior. Forgiveness
just allows you to move on.

398. You need to know you'll sometimes wonder who the lunatic is in your spouse's body. The trick is realizing the woman you married is in there . . . somewhere.

•

399. You need to know forgiveness oftentimes takes work: journaling, prayer, talking to someone, studying the Bible. If it was easy there would be no divorce.

•

400. You need to know it's perfectly OK to tell God that forgiveness isn't in your DNA so you need His help.

•

401. You need to know forgiveness has occurred when you're not churning inside anymore.

402. You need to know to not keep score.

•

403. You need to know that, in a strong marriage, forgiveness is a daily occurrence.

•

404. You need to know the only way to not stay hurt or angry is to forgive.

•

405. You need to know that if prayer alone doesn't help you forgive, maybe a therapist can.

•

406. You need to know few apologies are perfect. Don't dwell on how your spouse could have done better.

•

407. You need to know to get over it.

Marriage is Work

408. You need to know these stats:
   25% of marriages have to deal
      with alcoholism
   22% with drug addiction
   28% with infidelity
   40% with financial crisis
   100% with each other.

•

409. You need to know to act like you enjoy
what your spouse likes. She may love
watching the stars at night while you're
bored to tears. Still, you watch.

•

410. You need to know that if you
concentrate on what's good and right
and wonderful about your marriage,
soon that's all you'll be able to see.

411. You need to know shared sacrifice—
like tithing or community
service—makes a marriage stronger.

•

412. You need to know your
happiness can't rest on what your
spouse thinks of you this very moment.

•

413. You need to know God hasn't
assigned you to try and control your
spouse's thoughts. It's futile to try.

•

414. You need to know how to listen
without interrupting. It's real simple:
don't open your mouth.

415. You need to know the more
you practice acceptance, the happier
your marriage will be.

•

416. You need to know to develop
the gift of seeing things from
your spouse's point of view.

•

417. You need to know that once your
spouse believes you understand them,
your marriage will be stronger.

•

418. You need to know sometimes
even the best husbands and wives
weird out. Your life will be happier if
you don't make a big deal out of it.

419. You need to know a marriage
involves holidays with extended family.
Sometimes that means driving
across the country to have a burned
turkey dinner and listen to your spouse's
family argue about the will. Enjoy.

•

420. You need to know spending time
with the kids is good for the family.
But spending time alone with
each other is vital for the marriage.

•

421. You need to know you sometimes
have to get up from your La-Z-Boy,
take her hand, and go for a walk.

422. You need to know marriage is about compromise. Like he gets to watch Sunday night football if she gets to watch two hours of Animal Planet.

•

423. You need to know there'll be times when it's difficult to stand up to temptation. Like the temptation to throw away his favorite chair because you don't like looking at it. Don't do it.

•

424. You need to know to be willing to have those conversations that could lead to a fight, but are important to have. Like conversations about finances. Or job security. Or the children.

425. You need to know to be kind and gentle when you're talking on the phone with your spouse even when things are caving in at the office.

•

426. You need to know that listening to how your spouse's day went will sometimes require incredible willpower.

•

427. You need to know that time changes people. You vowed to stay *together*, not stay the *same*.

•

428. You need to know if you're not as attentive as you should be, they might be tempted to start flirting with other people.

429. You need to know how to listen
without comment or criticism or
judgment. Like when he expresses his love
for paintball fighting. Don't comment.

•

430. You need to know how
to listen without looking like you're
swallowing cough medicine.

•

431. You need to know that
a lasting marriage is based on
a couple's ability to resolve conflict.

•

432. You need to know he's not fighting
6:00 p.m. traffic jams just
to get home and immediately hear
how badly your day went. Give him
a chance to put on his hockey jersey.

433. You need to know if you,
a man, will agree with your wife, fights
can generally be averted. Unless she
thinks she looks fat. Use discretion.

•

434. You need to know to do what
you say you're going to do. Like, "I'll fold
the clothes at halftime." It helps
tremendously to follow through.

•

435. You need to know to never let her
do the dishes or clean the house alone.
You know, unless you're having surgery.
Or you've been kidnapped.

436. You need to know to ask yourself, "Would you rather be right or happy?" People who would rather be right end up in divorce court.

•

437. You need to know to ask for forgiveness. Don't let your pride get in the way of makeup sex.

•

438. You need to know a man just wants to solve the problem, women want to talk about how they feel. All night. Cavemen dealt with this.

439. You need to know to ask God to help you accept your spouse the way he or she is right now. That's a much more effective prayer than giving God a list of changes you want Him to make.

•

440. You need to know to ask God to help you change—to change your defensive attitudes, bad habits, and negative thoughts. You'll be amazed to find that He will.

•

441. You need to know it's important to remember why you got married in the first place. Remember why you couldn't live without each other.

442. You need to know hungry people are more difficult to be around than well-fed people. If they are acting cranky, it could be their blood sugar.

•

443. You need to know to not jump to conclusions. Like don't assume she's mad at you because she isn't talking. She could have lost a client, been embarrassed by her boss, or driven a screaming two-year-old around all day.

•

444. You need to know that when someone says they can walk away from you, show them the door. No marriage needs threats, coercion, or intimidation.

445. You need to know to do something kind for your spouse every day. And not get found out.

•

446. You need to know to accept his apology when it's offered. Even if you think he could have done better.

•

447. You need to know there are words that can cause irreparable damage. Use them cautiously.

•

448. You need to know the phrases "I'm sorry" and "I forgive you" tend to paralyze the lips of most people.

449. You need to know if you always fight to win, you could lose everything.

•

450. You need to know just because they're hostile doesn't mean you have to be. In fact, an argument can be avoided simply by not retaliating.

•

451. You need to know you can't control their moods, their fears, their spending, or their happiness. Trying to control anyone will actually cause more problems.

•

452. You need to know that if you work on your own issues instead of theirs, you'll both be happier.

453. You need to know to practice kindness, patience, and gentleness daily. It's hard at first, but gets easier.

•

454. You need to know that comparing him to more successful men is an excellent way for him to start comparing you to younger, better-looking women.

•

455. You need to know to remember these words, "You could be right."

•

456. You need to know that, despite what all the marriage books say, you don't need your spouse to be happy in order for you to be happy. Love him and pray for him. And let him work it out.

457. You need to know couples can learn to fight without tearing apart the fabric of the relationship.

•

458. You need to know a lot of problems can be solved by just asking for what you want. Like artichokes for dinner. No husband would ever guess that.

•

459. You need to know if you're marrying somebody with an addiction, saying "I do" won't make the addiction go away.

•

460. You need to know to keep flirting with each other. It's how all this got started.

461. You need to know the last thing
to trust in a marriage is your
feelings. You might feel like running
off to Siberia. Instead you need
to listen to her talk about her day.

•

462. You need to know research has
shown that happily married couples have
five times more positive thoughts than
negative thoughts about their spouses.
And you can control your thinking.

•

463. You need to know you can learn
to fall in love with someone again.

Marriage and Career

464. You need to know your marriage and career will compete for your attention.

•

465. You need to know to get your priorities in order: God. Family. Then work.

•

466. You need to know you could spend less than fifteen minutes a day talking to each other. If that happens, one day you won't recognize each other.

•

467. You need to know that your spouse will play a big role in your success at work.

•

468. You need to know to pay as much attention to your marriage as you do to your career.

469. You need to know to not make work your life. Some of the most successful businesspeople in the world are working on their third marriage.

•

470. You need to know to not make anyone feel guilty for going to work.

•

471. You need to know that wives with advanced degrees are at a greater risk for winding up single.

472. You need to know your most important business counselor is your spouse. In fact, most CEOs don't make an important decision unless they've talked it over with their husband or wife.

•

473. You need to know you don't have to go drinking with the gang after work. You need to go home.

•

474. You need to know that a budding career will mean long hours. And possibly weekend hours.

475. You need to know a working mother actually has seven jobs: she's a wife, a mother, a housekeeper, a chef, a nurse, a chauffeur, and an employee or employer.

•

476. You need to know to call home every day. Especially when you're traveling.

•

477. You need to know to not be jealous of the other women at the office. Suspicions will drive you crazy.

478. You need to know you may
have to move to advance in your career.
And to advance in their career,
your spouse may have to stay.

•

479. You need to know it could be you,
her, and her laptop in bed at night.

•

480. You need to know if your husband
works for you, it won't be easy to fire him.

•

481. You need to know that just because
the two of you can't work together
doesn't mean you don't love
each other. Few couples can actually
handle being together 24/7.

482. You need to know that both of you working at the same company can mean problems. A lot of couples thought working together at a large bank was a spectacularly good idea. Suddenly no one in the family had a job.

•

483. You need to know to discuss what boundaries you're comfortable with as a couple before one of you has to work and travel with the opposite sex.

•

484. You need to know that, in a growing number of marriages, men no longer make the most money. Yet they still don't know how to fold laundry.

485. You need to know a wife takes her husband's job loss harder than he does.

•

486. You need to know that if you both retire at the same time, you'll be happier. The alternative is a spouse who resents getting up at 6:30 a.m. to go to work while the other one sleeps in.

•

487. You need to know, if you took time off from your career to raise kids, not to blame your husband that the job market is more difficult to enter than it was ten years ago.

488. You need to know that sometimes you live in one town and work on the other side of the country. Almost four million couples now live in commuter marriages.

•

489. You need to know if you and your spouse have different work hours, it will seem like you're in a commuter marriage.

Marriage and Intimacy

490. You need to know being married means you have somebody to tell your secrets to.

●

491. You need to know you're the one person in the world they trust to not hurt them.

●

492. You need to know praying together can be more intimate than sex. And just as important for a healthy marriage.

●

493. You need to know there are five kinds of intimacy: physical, emotional, mental, social, and the easiest and quickest, the physical.

494. You need to know to hold hands like teenagers do. In the movies, walking down the street, in restaurants.

•

495. You need to know sometimes you're the strong one. Sometimes not.

•

496. You need to know that dreaming about the future together is one of the real joys of marriage. He may dream about a monster pickup truck; she may dream about shutters. Enjoy the dreams.

497. You need to know being married doesn't mean you stop dating each other. In fact, it's more important than ever to have date nights.

•

498. You need to know the closer you grow to somebody, the greater the potential for pain is. This is one reason why some people pull away.

•

499. You need to know one peculiar joy of marriage is to be able to hug and kiss knowing nothing else will happen.

500. You need to know a marriage grows stale if all you do is meet each other's expectations.

•

501. You need to know that having fun is as important as sharing responsibilities.

•

502. You need to know the more time you dwell on how wonderful your marriage is, the more wonderful it will become.

•

503. You need to know that writing love notes works as well now as it did twenty years ago when you were dating.

504. You need to know how important it is to smile at each other. It's far superior to frowning when you make eye contact.

•

505. You need to know to dance in the kitchen while the pasta boils.

•

506. You need to know you can still go on cheap dates. The point is being together.

•

507. You need to know you can do something new without leaving the house. Like spend the night in another bedroom.

508. You need to know to not put on the oldest, rattiest things you own every night when you get home.

•

509. You need to know there are few aphrodisiacs in the world more powerful than just listening.

•

510. You need to know to spend time hugging each other in bed in the mornings. It sets a nice tone for the day.

Marriage and
Children

511. You need to know the relationship with your children can never be more important than your marriage.

•

512. You need to know experts suggest waiting a year or two before having kids so the two of you can grow in your relationship.

•

513. You need to know having children is actually more life changing than getting married.

514. You need to know she'll want to have a deep meaningful discussion about whether Brook is a boy's name or a girl's name. With about two minutes to go in a tight game.

•

515. You need to know a child won't save your marriage. That's a lot of responsibility to put on a three-month-old.

•

516. You need to know that even if he dresses the kids for school, packs the lunchboxes, and writes the thank-you notes, she will always feel like she's the one being judged by the world.

•

517. You need to know fathers need to take parental leave as much as moms do.

518. You need to know children can put a marriage at risk. The pressure, the fears, the finances, the late nights— these aren't romance enhancers.

●

519. You need to know it's easy for new moms to get so into being a mom they forget their husbands want to be part of the baby's life too.

●

520. You need to know that, in spite of best-laid plans, the burden of childcare falls primarily on the parent who can breastfeed.

521. You need to know that
shared parenting—where each
partner has equal tasks—is a nice ideal.
But if he's a firefighter pulling
72-hour shifts, she's going to assume
most of the childcare responsibilities.

•

522. You need to know gender shouldn't
determine who does daily childcare tasks.
Who's going to feed them, bathe them,
and make sure they don't stick
a nail file into the electric sockets
will depend on who's home.

523. You need to know marital happiness tends to plummet for a new mom. Husbands bearing gifts, showing kindness, extending patience, and being home a lot help restore a new mom's balance.

•

524. You need to know couples argue about children—how much they cost, who's going to take care of them, and what their ground rules will be.

•

525. You need to know the earlier you make plans, the better. Decide who will earn the income, who will do the dishes, who will change the baby and when, who gets to sleep at night, who gets to wake up, etc. Making these decisions now can avoid a lot of 3:00 a.m. arguments.

526. You need to know the two of you don't have all the answers. Hey, you may only have two or three answers. Each needs their own support network.

•

527. You need to know having children means deciding whether you can live on one income or if you'll need two.

•

528. You need to know you get to rub your wife's back for nine months during pregnancy. Don't think she'll remember this. No, it's not fair.

•

529. You need to know your children should be adored. But your spouse must come first.

530. You need to know that when she's pregnant, he should meet the doctors. Let her know she has a man who cares.

•

531. You need to know that if she takes medication for postpartum disorder, it won't make her into a drug addict. It means she won't have crying spells, be moody, and become depressed. Husbands can help by being kind, patient, and available.

•

532. You need to know some loving couples simply can't conceive a child. So, in a stupendous act of faith, they adopt. And they learn this was the child God had intended for them all along. Oftentimes, the baby even looks like Mom or Dad! Go figure.

533. You need to know if two people are working ten hours a day to make ends meet, a baby will not make life easier.

•

534. You need to know that, when expecting, he'll want to spend weekends biking or golfing or hanging out with friends. She'll want to spend weekends shopping at baby stores.

•

535. You need to know that constantly attending to a baby can make the pressures, politics, and meetings at the office look good.

536. You need to know a baby
means you can no longer afford
the lifestyle you used to have.

•

537. You need to know it takes two people
to put a crib together. Block out the day.

•

538. You need to know a colicky three-
month-old baby will leave you too
exhausted to talk, much less fool around.

•

539. You need to know sleep is one
of those things parents do without.
For the first eighteen years or so.

540. You need to know parenthood
is a lot about teamwork.

•

541. You need to know there will be days
when you're so tired of little hands
touching you that you don't even want to
touch each other. This is temporary.

•

542. You need to know a babysitter
may be the most important
person in your marriage.

•

543. You need to know that while it seems
like kids cost a fortune, it's actually the
first one who costs a fortune. The rest
of them get hand-me-downs.

544. You need to know one way
to spend more time with your husband
when you have children is to
spend less time on the housework.

•

545. You need to know your children's
teachers can tell the difference between
a child from a stable marriage and
a child from a rocky one.

•

546. You need to know having
a baby before marriage
doesn't strengthen relationships.

547. You need to know you'll talk to each other in a whole new language with words like *poop, coooooookie, susho shusho, dah,* and *nanna.* You're not regressing. You're parents.

•

548. You need to know a father will worry about his children's ability to make it in the world. Moms will always worry about their happiness.

•

549. You need to know from the beginning who is going to raise your children. Him? Her? Daycare? The mother-in-law?

550. You need to know moms tend to spend everything on the kids while the dads tend to panic over of the price of diapers. Communication is vital here.

•

551. You need to know to never tell your kids you're so mad you could divorce their father. It makes you sound like a lunatic. And it scares them to death.

•

552. You need to know to buy a lock for your bedroom. Marriage saver.

553. You need to know to make the hard decisions together. Then stand by them.

•

554. You need to know to totally agree about homework, chores, money, and show respect when you're in front of your kids. Settle any differences behind closed doors.

•

555. You need to know that neither spouse should encourage a three-year-old to misbehave.

•

556. You need to know there's no such thing as a romantic dinner when a two-year-old is involved.

557. You need to know that where you once discussed music and fashion and your jobs, you now discuss pooping. As well as the color of snot and how to get barf stains out of a shirt.

•

558. You need to know that one parent shouldn't always be the bad guy. Both parents need to enforce the rules.

•

559. You need to know to never criticize each other in front of the kids.

560. You need to know a spouse
who constantly undermines
the other's abilities as a parent
isn't doing the marriage any favors.

•

561. You need to know your children's
health—physical, emotional,
and otherwise—depends on
the health of your marriage.

•

562. You need to know God has made
you responsible for teaching your kids
about marriage and relationships.

•

563. You need to know your sexual
relationship will sometimes depend
on Saturday morning cartoons.

564. You need to know to always agree in front of your children. This gives a six-year-old no opening.

●

565. You need to know a mother will always wonder if her child has pooped today. This never crosses a man's mind.

●

566. You need to know exhaustion is a byproduct of children.

●

567. You need to know children are better off when either Mom or Dad stays home. Sacrifices may be in order.

568. You need to know a stay-at-home mom
needs a vacation as much as a
dad who works twelve hours a day.

•

569. You need to know nothing prepares
you as a couple for the teenage years.
Except maybe military duty.

•

570. You need to know it's important
to get away. Just the two of you.
Even to a Motel 6 down the street.

•

571. You need to know some of your
biggest fights will be over how
much money to give the kids. Dads
generally want to give them zero.
Moms want to give them Montana.

572. You need to know you'll be
funding college about the time
you'll need to be funding retirement.

•

573. You need to know you don't have to
invite your adult kids to join you every time
you go out to dinner. Moms forget this.

•

574. You need to know your retirement
account will shrink if you continue to
support your twenty-something kids.

•

575. You need to know adult kids moving
home can bring a couple closer. Or it can
seem like your marriage has been invaded
by expensive, oversize teenagers.

576. You need to know even an adult kid's actions can put a strain on a marriage. This is why your marriage has to come first.

•

577. You need to know it takes two people to let go of a child just as much as it takes two people to raise one.

•

578. You need to know you can't fix your adult child's marriage just because you're . . . well . . . married.

•

579. You need to know that the best way to love your kids is to love each other.

580. You need to know that, when the kids leave home, you'll have plenty to talk about. Like what just happened the last twenty years.

•

581. You need to know the "empty nest syndrome" lasts about ten minutes. Really.

•

582. You need to know they might come back.

Marriage and Money

583. You need to know love won't pay the mortgage. Money is important.

•

584. You need to know if you're marrying a spender or a saver.

•

585. You need to know a marriage is a merging of two financial lifestyles. One could be the Salvation Army; the other, Chanel.

•

586. You need to know it's cheaper to get married in November and January. Yet you get the same ending as the June weddings do.

•

587. You need to know financial security eliminates a lot of arguments.

588. You need to know if you don't
buy stuff you can't afford,
you won't have financial problems.

•

589. You need to know that if you put
$30,000 on your credit card to get married,
you'll have money problems from day one.

•

590. You need to know to have financial
discussions before you say "I do."

•

591. You need to know to share your
credit reports. Get them from Equifax,
TransUnion and Experian. This way both
parties know what they're getting into.

592. You need to know a credit report
is the easiest way to tell
how a person handles money.

•

593. You need to know people are often
more open with their bodies than
they are about their financial situations.

•

594. You need to know if your
fiancé won't talk about money,
you're going to have big problems.

•

595. You need to know that if you're
marrying a person with high credit
card bills or college expenses, those
debts will become your problem.

596. You need to know to develop a set of rules that will govern your financial behavior. Rules about not yelling at each other, not making accusations, no impulse buying—these are things you must agree on for financial and marital peace.

•

597. You need to know to agree that neither one of you spends more than $150 without telling the other. Even if you have separate accounts.

•

598. You need to know that major purchases can be a financial strain if there's no budget or plan. And a major resentment if both parties don't agree.

599. You need to know money problems break up more marriages than infidelity does. And often even that's caused by money issues.

•

600. You need to know one of the great predictors of wealth is a solid marriage.

•

601. You need to know that if he grew up overindulged, then he will feel entitled to the best of everything, whether or not you two can afford it.

•

602. You need to know that if she grew up scrimping and saving, then she'll worry all the time about not having enough.

603. You need to know how your spouse feels about credit cards: should they be paid off every month, or should a balance be carried forward?

•

604. You need to know that if the two of you make a lot of money and don't communicate, your problems will be that much more expensive.

•

605. You need to know to invest in software like Quicken. It tells you where the money's going.

•

606. You need to know there should be no secret bank accounts. It's weird, it's lying by omission, and can instill a lack of trust.

607. You need to know the power of compounding interest. It means regular little deposits can make you rich over thirty or forty years. Talk to your financial adviser.

•

608. You need to know that each of you should have an IRA.

•

609. You need to know you can avoid most financial emergencies and arguments by having enough savings to ride out the bad times.

•

610. You need to know a lot of fights about money can be avoided by making a budget. You can find tons of information about creating one online.

611. You need to know that each of you
should have some mad money
to spend without explanation.

•

612. You need to know to pay bills
together. This keeps one person
from being scared to death while
the other person lives in a fantasyland.

•

613. You need to know that just because
your wife is in finance doesn't mean she
will be good managing the checkbook.

•

614. You need to know not only
your spouse's financial habits
and goals but also your own.

615. You need to know each other's tolerance of risk: one person may want to invest in oil wells while the other one thinks CDs are too volatile.

•

616. You need to know that having a pile of money doesn't keep you from being a miserable couple.

•

617. You need to know that a good financial counselor can keep you from making an appointment with a marriage counselor.

•

618. You need to know if one of you is thinking there should be a stay-at-home parent. And what the financial impact of that would be.

619. You need to know that sometimes life and finances will require you to downsize.

•

620. You need to know that establishing a budget and then sticking to it means you don't have to lie awake at night worrying about money. You can lie awake at night worrying about other things.

•

621. You need to know to not budget for the best of times, but the worst of times. Then during the best of times you can save. And during the worst of times you can survive.

•

622. You need to know money comes and goes. Couples in stable marriages handle it.

623. You need to know that if
you live below your means,
money will not be an issue.

•

624. You need to know to budget for the
unexpected. The computer breaking, the
doctor's bill being double what you
thought, the brakes wearing out—they
could all happen in the same week.

•

625. You need to know there's a difference
between a regular savings account (the
future) and an emergency savings account
(a broken water pipe in your attic).

•

626. You need to know you need six
months of expenses tucked away in
an emergency savings account.

627. You need to know you don't need a lot
of money to start saving. Just
a lot of agreement. And willpower.

•

628. You need to know it's important to
regularly discuss your financial situation.

•

629. You need to know to do estate planning
along with your wedding planning.

•

630. You need to know to pray
for wisdom about money.

•

631. You need to know that when
things get tough financially,
God hasn't departed the scene.

632. You need to know to establish upper limits on spending—and to stick to them. Like the upper limit on children's Christmas gifts. The upper limit for birthday parties. This keeps one parent from being knocked over by a $250 pair of sneakers.

•

633. You need to know if one person spends like there's no tomorrow, the other person will be scared to death.

•

634. You need to know poverty can be a marriage killer.

635. You need to know the spending habits he has when he's twenty-five will not be substantially different when he's fifty-five.

•

636. You need to know the IRS takes a dim view of unreported income and tends to blame both people.

•

637. You need to know financial crises are gut-wrenching, agonizing, and— most importantly—survivable.

•

638. You need to know it's childish to try to outspend each other in the name of fairness. ("You spent $2,000 on a refrigerator, so I'm buying $2,000 golf clubs.")

639. You need to know that money, used wisely, can pay for a nice house, food on the table, college for the kids, and make other people's lives better.

•

640. You need to know you don't need a lot of money to furnish a home or apartment. You need Craigslist, eBay, and IKEA.

•

641. You need to know being married to a rich person who's unfaithful, argumentative, and depressed will make you realize money isn't everything.

•

642. You need to know your kids will think your money is their money.

643. You need to know that if you start saving from the first paycheck, saving will be much easier ten years down the road.

•

644. You need to know money can help make you happy. And giving it away makes you happier.

•

645. You need to know you can check your credit report every twelve months for free at www.annualcreditreport.com. Then, when you go to buy a house, there will be no surprises.

•

646. You need to know to buy life insurance. Yes, it's the price of satellite TV, but it means your family can keep their home if something happens to you.

647. You need to know you can get solid advice on credit and financial problems at www.debtadvice.org.

•

648. You need to know couples who give money back to God at the beginning of the month find they have more money than they expected at the end of each month.

•

649. You need to know there could be fights over whether or not to tithe.

•

650. You need to know financial security begins with the realization that it's all God's money. He's just giving you some to manage.

Marriage Counseling

651. You need to know the secret to a strong, healthy marriage is two strong, healthy individuals. It's difficult to repair a marriage if one person is nuts.

•

652. You need to know that when you'd prefer working on sales reports until 8:00 p.m. instead of going home, it's time to seek counseling.

•

653. You need to know if you'd rather sit in your car than go inside and see your wife, it's time to seek counseling.

•

654. You need to know if you haven't had sex in three months, it's time to seek counseling.

655. You need to know if you feel like hitting her, it's time to seek counseling.

•

656. You need to know that if you can't be kind to each other, it's time to seek counseling.

•

657. You need to know that if you think your husband is a failure, it's time seek counseling.

•

658. You need to know that if you're fighting over the utility bills, it's time to seek counseling.

659. You need to know that if dirty laundry is causing you to blow a gasket, get a maid. Really, it's much cheaper than divorce court.

•

660. You need to know there are a million therapists out there, and it's okay to shop around. When you find the right one, you'll both know.

•

661. You need to know that if you don't want to spill your guts to a therapist, a marriage education program can work wonders. Check out www.smartmarriages.com.

662. You need to know the American Association for Marriage and Family Therapy can help you find a therapist in your area (www.aamft.org).

•

663. You need to know that if your biggest complaint is that your meals aren't ready when you get home, you don't need couples counseling. Electroshock therapy is what's needed.

•

664. You need to know that if one person refuses to go to marriage counseling, the other one should still go. Working on yourself never hurts.

665. You need to know a good counselor may not be able to save a bad marriage.

•

666. You need to know if your marriage counselor is divorced.

•

667. You need to know if going to the same counselor for six months hasn't helped, it's time to find a new counselor.

Marriage and Fidelity

668. You need to know where each
of you stands on sexual fidelity.
You think you know. But make sure.

•

669. You need to know an affair
is more likely to affect your
marriage than a divorce. And that
happens to 50 percent of marriages.

•

670. You need to know you can
no longer fantasize about
other people. Really. It's stupid.

•

671. You need to know that studies
indicate the more sexual partners
a person has before marriage, the
more likely that person is to stray.

672. You need to know an affair doesn't just happen. It's a decision you make along the way.

•

673. You need to know research strongly suggests an affair doesn't make you happier. Even if no one finds out.

•

674. You need to know an affair won't do anything for your self-esteem. Except ruin it.

•

675. You need to know an affair won't make you feel more beautiful.

676. You need to know it's stupid to use an unsatisfactory sex life as a reason for fooling around. Your partner is having as bad a time as you are.

•

677. You need to know the reactions of a betrayed spouse resemble those of a soldier after coming home from combat: complete shock.

•

678. You need to know that husbands and wives under forty are equally capable of straying.

•

679. You need to know that even in so-called "open marriages," infidelity leads to rage, jealousy, and abandonment fears.

680. You need to know that your adultery
isn't your spouse's fault.

•

681. You need to know to look at each other
with the same passion and interest as you
did ten years ago. The looks of "Did you
pay the mortgage?" and "I'm stumbling
over your shoes" do nothing for romance.

•

682. You need to know therapists
recommend talking to your spouse
about being attracted to another
person before you do something stupid.
It lessens the likelihood of
having to talk to a lawyer later.

683. You need to know if you're drinking without your husband around, any idiot could look good after several hours.

•

684. You need to know the more you know about each other's past, the better able you'll be to withstand the present strains.

•

685. You need to know you can always walk away from an affair before it gets started. Even if it means going home to a stressed-out mom of two babies.

•

686. You need to know women tend to stray because of their need to connect to a man emotionally. Men who don't understand this wind up watching ESPN alone. Real alone.

687. You need to know that having one affair will tend to lead to another.

•

688. You need to know that an affair means your spouse can never trust you again. She may forgive you. She may go to counseling. She can pray for hours on end. But trust has been shattered.

Marriage and Chores

689. You need to know a husband doing housework is a turn-on for women.

•

690. You need to know who's going to push the vacuum cleaner and who's going to take out the garbage. You better believe the issue will come up.

•

691. You need to know whoever works at home is expected to keep the place clean. Even if they are the primary breadwinner.

•

692. You need to know that even when a wife goes to work and her husband tends the house, she still does most of the housework. It's not a plot. It's reality.

693. You need to know that a successful division of housework depends on what your friends are doing. Husbands will copy other husbands.

•

694. You need to know a woman can see dirt two or three days before a man does.

•

695. You need to know that for some weird reason, women don't equate washing the car or changing light bulbs with folding the laundry or scrubbing the toilets.

•

696. You need to know research indicates 59% of men lose their hearing when a woman asks them to clean the house.

697. You need to know the more you tell him he didn't do housework right the more he'll let you do it by yourself.

•

698. You need to know there's no such thing as men's chores and women's chores. That kind of thinking puts men on the couch for the night.

•

699. You need to know there's a difference between obsession and housework. If you're obsessed with keeping everything spotless, don't expect him to share your enthusiasm for Windexing.

700. You need to know a man's inclination is to put things off, while a woman's is to strike before the sun's up. That's why she's vacuuming while he's groggily looking for the coffeemaker.

●

701. You need to know that when he actually does clean the house, he wants to be praised like he's coming home from battle.

●

702. You need to know if someone feels like they're doing all the work in a marriage, the marriage is in trouble.

●

703. You need to know a dishwasher isn't a birthday gift. It's an appliance.

Marriage and
In-Laws

704. You need to know that every family has issues. Even if everything looks perfectly wonderful from the outside.

•

705. You need to know that marriage fundamentally changes your relationship with your parents.

•

706. You need to know your husband's ideas are now more important than your mom's.

•

707. You need to know you have to get along with her family even though she's told you her father was abusive and her mother hears voices. Happy Thanksgiving.

708. You need to know to not let parents buy you too many gifts. They usually come with strings. And guilt.

•

709. You need to know you shouldn't try and change your wife because your parents believe she could use some improvement.

•

710. You need to know your own family, no matter what you think, teeters on mental instability.

•

711. You need to know your mother-in-law will give you some really screwy gifts. Thank her warmly and re-gift them to your cousin's neighbor's housesitter.

712. You need to know you now have to schedule who you'll have holiday meals with. And that might mean two Thanksgiving dinners in six hours.

•

713. You need to know she probably doesn't want to be compared to her mother. Compare her to Attila the Hun. Compare her to the plague. Just leave out her mother.

•

714. You need to know to stay out of family feuds. You'll be seeing these same people during the holidays, and they'll remember that you yelled at them.

715. You need to know that if his mom is
an addict, your marriage
will be that much more interesting.

•

716. You need to know that if
you're marrying someone whose
parents are practicing alcoholics,
chances are strong something is
off the rails in your family too.

•

717. You need to know to send
your mother-in-law flowers every
now and then. Untold benefits.

718. You need to know to not tell your mom about every fight. You'll get over it and make up. She won't.

•

719. You need to know you'll have to be strong enough to tell your dad to butt out. Your spouse is the most important person in your life now.

•

720. You need to know your parents don't mean to get in the way. They think they're helping.

•

721. You need to know just one word when it comes to appreciating parents and in-laws: babysitters.

722. You need to know you might spend more time and money taking care of your parents than your kids.

•

723. You need to know if he wants to live near Mom or if he'd be willing to move to Utah for your career.

•

724. You need to know that at about the same time your kids are leaving home, his parents could be moving in.

Second Marriage

725. You need to know being married again means you were blessed to find comfort and companionship again.

•

726. You need to know that it is totally possible to get it completely wrong the first time, and completely right the second.

•

727. You need to know marriage is a sacrament. Even second marriages. Even fourth marriages.

•

728. You need to know a second marriage often means feeling like a teenager when you . . . well . . . have teenagers.

729. You need to know to make a final emotional divorce from your ex in order to clear the path for your new marriage.

•

730. You need to know a second marriage presents you with new financial complications: houses, retirement accounts, insurance policies, and . . . of course . . . kids.

•

731. You need to know the chances are good that problems from your first marriage will carry into your second marriage.

732. You need to know if fear
and resentment from your first
marriage are complicating the
second, it's time to seek counseling.

•

733. You need to know a second
marriage means your children
can have a part in your wedding. But
they may not want to. Let them decide.

•

734. You need to know your
children and your fiancé's children
may harbor fantasies of their parents
getting back together. Go slowly.

735. You need to know 65% of remarriages include children from previous families.

·

736. You need to know your children may not be all that thrilled with the possibility of living with a stepparent.

·

737. You need to know you're not going to fall in love with your partner's children overnight. In fact, it may take a while.

·

738. You need to know your stepchildren aren't going to fall in love with you because you're a nice person who gives them money.

739. You need to know it's your job
to get to know your spouse's
children. And to earn their respect.

•

740. You need to know you'll
struggle with who comes first:
your kids or your new spouse.

•

741. You need to know your children and
their children may never be close friends.
But, over time, everybody can learn to
respect and tolerate one another.

•

742. You need to know twins can fight
like cats and dogs. So it's normal
for stepbrothers and stepsisters
to have fallings-out.

743. You need to know you're not Cinderella's stepmother. You're not wicked.

•

744. You need to know that moving into a new home for a fresh start might be easier for everyone.

•

745. You need to know you'll be tempted to show favoritism to your stepchildren. Then you'll feel so guilty you'll want to buy your own child a car. But he's only twelve.

•

746. You need to know the relationship you have with your spouse's kids while you're dating will change when you get married. Inevitably.

747. You need to know that, for a while,
the stepparent shouldn't be
your kids' disciplinarian.

•

748. You need to know to decide
up-front who's paying for what (the
mortgage, vacations, private
soccer lessons) and for how long.

•

749. You need to know to make special
arrangements for stepkids who visit
a few days each week or month. Make
sure they have their own bed, toothbrush,
toiletries, and clothes so they feel like
members of the family. Not visitors.

750. You need to know to wait until you've
bonded as a family before
you have a new baby together. The
children's nerves are frayed enough.

•

751. You need to know the moment you
start referring to the children
as "my kids" and "your kids,"
you're entering deep water.

•

752. You need to know some things never
change, and that includes disagreements
over money, noise, discipline, and other
everyday ups and downs of family life.

•

753. You need to know keeping
your emotions bottled up didn't
work in your first marriage.

754. You need to know a new marriage isn't going to solve your kids' problems. Kids in new families have the same issues as kids in single-parent divorced homes.

•

755. You need to know it's important to spend time just with your own kids. They need you now more than ever.

•

756. You need to know to decide who makes emergency medical decisions for your kids if you're not around. Your ex? Your spouse? Your father?

757. You need to know a will protects your children, but be sure to address the fact that a surviving spouse might be entitled to your estate. Cutting out your kids.

•

758. You need to know it's a good idea to keep separate personal accounts, but to pool cost-of-living money in a joint account. This is what the rich and famous do.

•

759. You need to know your stepkids will probably like their grandparents (her ex in-laws) more than they like you. Perfectly normal.

760. You need to know that if
you bring children into a marriage,
you're going to have to be deliberate
about making time for your marriage.
Doing so will only benefit your kids.

761. You need to know teenagers can be
sullen, moody, difficult, and frustrating
even when there's not a stepparent in their
lives. You're not the cause.

762. You need to know your stepkids will
decide what to call you. They may not be
comfortable with "Mom" or "Dad."

763. You need to know to encourage your stepchildren to have close relationships with *both* their birth parents.

•

764. You need to know your new family needs new traditions.

•

765. You need to know special occasions involving children now include you, your new spouse, your ex spouse, everybody's stepchildren, and everybody's parents.

•

766. You need to know to stay active in your children's lives, especially if they don't live with you.

767. You need to know that, even after you remarry, the pain over the end of your first marriage may take a long, long time to go away.

•

768. You need to know why the first marriage didn't work. So you can make sure this one will.

•

769. You need to know his ex mother-in-law might call. Regularly.

Dealing with
a Woman

770. You need to remember these four words: "Your hair looks great."

●

771. You need to know she wants to talk. A lot. Sometimes about the kids. Sometimes about a book she's reading. Sometimes about work. Sometimes when all you want is quiet. Sometimes about stuff you've already talked about—several times before.

●

772. You need to know women come with hormones.

●

773. You need to know you have assumed the responsibility of protecting her, caring for her, and providing for her in the physical, mental, sexual, emotional, and spiritual areas of her life.

774. You need to know your job isn't more important than hers.

•

775. You need to know she needs you to be present mentally when you're there physically.

•

776. You need to know there is a rule, written down somewhere, that says fathers must take their children for donuts on Saturday morning while mom sleeps in. Don't bother trying to find it. Just follow it.

•

777. You need to know there will be days when her hormones will be in control of her mind. Love her anyway.

778. You need to know her definition of "shopping" doesn't include buying clothes for the kids, cosmetics, groceries, pots and pans or buying appliances. Those are necessities. Actually "shopping" is hard to pin down.

•

779. You need to know women feel it their duty to buy presents for every birthday, anniversary, Christmas, and wedding for everyone in their family. And their friends. And their kids' friends.

•

780. You need to know she still likes it when you open doors for her.

•

781. You need to know to say "yes" more than you say "no." This is hard for men.

782. You need to know she'll keep 92 products on the counter for her to look like she doesn't wear makeup. Yes, they're in the way. No, don't touch them.

•

783. You need to know she really won't buy into the notion that men are the stronger sex until there's a noise in the house at 2 a.m.

•

784. You need to know that, for some reason, she'll think the pair of shoes that make her feet hurt the worst look the best on her. There's nothing you can say.

•

785. You need to know she doesn't want to compete with a game console.

786. You need to know you can't make her happy all the time, you can't please her all the time, and you can't understand her all the time. You can, however, love her all the time.

•

787. You need to know that if you leave the toilet seat up only one time, that will be the night she staggers to the bathroom at 2:00 a.m. and plops down in the toilet. You won't be able to run far enough.

•

788. You need to know women fantasize about divorce if they feel they do a majority of the housework. It doesn't matter if you're a CEO. She wants you to help fold clothes.

789. You need to know she'll put on lipstick before bedtime. She wants to look good going to sleep.

•

790. You need to know to hold her hand when she wouldn't expect it. Like in a football stadium.

•

791. You need to know to not try to control her spending. She's an adult.

•

792. You need to know a woman feels loved when she's cared for.

•

793. You need to know that the sound of you going to the bathroom and brushing your teeth at the same time scares her.

794. You need to know she'll feel jealous if she thinks you're ignoring her to talk to a pretty woman. She'll say she's not jealous. Then she won't say another word the rest of the night.

•

795. You need to know you can't fix an angry woman. You can listen to her, feed her, agree with her, and listen to her some more. Try and fix her, and it will be your fault.

•

796. You need to know she's not fooled when you try to kiss her and keep your eyes on the TV at the same time.

797. You need to know she likes your making passes at her. In fact, if you don't, she'll wonder what's wrong.

•

798. You need to know if you get in her bathtub, not to touch her bubble bath, skin softener, candles, soap, body bath, loofah, moisturizer, bath pouf, bath salts, bath potions, sponge, or her exfoliating glove. Really it would be best to just stay away.

•

799. You need to know her emery board is not to be used on your feet in bed.

800. You need to know she secretly believes that if you use her razor on your face, you will give her a staph infection. Somehow though, your razor is perfectly safe for her legs.

•

801. You need to know she won't appreciate the *Sports Illustrated* swimsuit edition like you do.

•

802. You need to know she's not going to wear revealing lingerie around the house all the time. Only in your dreams.

•

803. You need to know you can't buy her happiness. So have a plan B.

804. You need to know if she has a fight with her mom, don't take sides. In fact, go outside.

•

805. You need to know that if she's criticizing another woman, you're safest play is to smile and agree.

•

806. You need to know that what women want from their husbands is confidence that everything is going to be all right.

•

807. You need to know she might not like all your friends. In fact, if she likes one or two of them, count yourself lucky.

808. You need to know that you looking like Arnold Schwarzenegger will be much more important to you than to her.

•

809. You need to know a woman's intrinsic nature is to guard her nest. Anything that threatens that nest will turn her into an enraged, furious, AK-47 packing kamikaze pilot. It's best to get out of the way.

•

810. You need to know diapers don't smell any better to her.

•

811. You need to know if she's not into sports, you'll have to explain the rules. Many women find football as difficult to comprehend as men do *La Bohéme*.

812. You need to know she married you to be with you. Not to get calls from the duck blind.

•

813. You need to know that what the Bible says about the way you treat your wife impacts how God answers your prayers. 1 Peter 3:7. Look it up.

•

814. You need to know to watch her dumb romantic movies, especially if she watches your dumb violent ones.

•

815. You need to know that she wants you to be able to make a decision. Seriously.

816. You need to know to
take her shopping and buy her
outfits she would never buy for herself.

•

817. You need to know that just
because she goes to your football,
baseball, and basketball games doesn't
necessarily mean she likes them.
She may just like being with you.

•

818. You need to know googling
"estrogen" will help explain
what's happening to your life.

•

819. You need to know she likes dessert.
She doesn't want to be asked if she
wants it. She just wants you to order it.

820. You need to know she needs
her own group of friends.
They can save your marriage.

•

821. You need to know to hug
her even when she's mad and
telling you not to touch her.

•

822. You need to know to buy her
a diamond. Even if you have to wait
twenty years to afford the right one.

•

823. You need to know that, for some
reason, women aren't huge fans of movies
than involve explosions, car chases,
helicopters, gunfights, karate, or girls
in swimsuits. Yes, that's weird.

824. You need to know women like to make lists. And just when you think everything on that list is checked off, she'll make another list.

•

825. You need to know she's not going to want to name her child after a state, a motorcycle, or an English soccer team.

•

826. You need to know that just because she's a she, she may not know how to sew.

•

827. You need to know you can't wash your jeans and shorts with her underwear. Who knows why. . . .

•

828. You need to know it's not always her hormones. You might actually be at fault.

829. You need to know that women, for some reason, care that the bed is made.

•

830. You need to know to talk to her about more things than how tough your day was and that she's spending too much money.

•

831. You need to know that lighting a scented candle before she wakes up sets a nice tone for the day.

•

832. You need to know she will paint the house the color she likes. Your best move is to smile and nod.

•

833. You need to know how to clean the kitchen. Really, life will be smoother.

834. You need to know that she needs to know she's the most important thing in your life. For some reason, that's easy for women to forget.

•

835. You need to know to make a pass at her when you're at the movies. Of course you'll get shot down, but you knew the odds were slim anyway.

•

836. You need to know she'd like you to change T-shirts. In fact, it may be time to throw that fifteen-year-old shirt away.

•

837. You need to know your feet, your gym socks, and your tennis shoes smell. Don't take it personally when she mentions it.

838. You need to know when she screams at you to slow down, she's not criticizing. She's afraid of pain and death.

•

839. You need to know the answer to the question "Do I look fat?" is always "No." Always. Always. (For extra credit, you could add, "Actually, I think you could use a few more pounds.")

•

840. You need to know if you're upset because dinner isn't ready when you get home, you haven't spent enough time doing your wife's job.

841. You need to know she will be stunned to come home to a candlelight dinner served on the fine china. So stunned that amazing things will happen later in the evening.

•

842. You need to know that a wife who feels taken for granted is a wife who may start looking for another man who makes her feel desirable and wanted.

•

843. You need to know the answer to her question "What are you thinking?" should always, always, always be "How beautiful you are."

•

844. You need to know to send her flowers with a truly sappy card for no real reason.

845. You need to know any wife who asks, "Do you love me?" wants a one-word answer. Don't elaborate. ("Yes, though I wish you'd cut your hair like the trainee in legal . . ." Don't go there.)

•

846. You need to know from this point on no other girl is pretty. The very best looking are "not bad."

•

847. You need to use deodorant. And floss.

•

848. You need to know she will care deeply about things that mystify you. Like accent pillows. And bedspreads. Don't ask.

849. You need to know she thinks
your back and chest are too hairy.
And she wants to shave them.

•

850. You need to know watching a sunset
instead of TV can help you learn more
about what's going on with her.

•

851. You need to know to buy her
an extravagant gift every now
and then for no reason at all. It says
all the things you've neglected to.
It might make up for taking her
to Hooters on your anniversary.

852. You need to know she'll want to talk about her feelings: her feelings about the future, her feelings about spaghetti, her feelings about her ex best friend in junior high. Though you'd rather pull out your teeth one at a time, sit down and listen.

•

853. You need to know that even though she loves you, you could use some improvement. Like your clothes. Who bought them for you? Your *ex girlfriend*?

•

854. You need to know that, unless requested, she doesn't want your help in the kitchen. Just your company.

855. You need to know a perfectly sane woman can have seven different moods in one hour. You can't control them. Heck, she can't even control them.

•

856. You need to know you're living with a person who can tear up over a Toyota commercial.

•

857. You need to know there's something genetic in a woman that makes her cook soup when you or your kids are sick.

•

858. You need to know that, even after twenty-five years, she'll still sometimes worry if you really love her.

859. You need to know that in any twenty-four-hour period, she could be worried about finances, about her parents enjoying retirement, about her children's refusal to get married, about her dog's happiness and about your apparent blindness to dirty clothes on the floor. One right after another.

•

860. You need to know you're going to like her new haircut. Even though you haven't seen it. You like it.

•

861. You need to know that if she's crying because she doesn't like her new haircut and color, it's a good idea to hand her another $100 to have it redone. Trust me on this.

862. You need to know when your adult kids come home to visit, she will mother them like they're ten years old. If she didn't, they wouldn't come home.

•

863. You need to know to smile and nod when she says she always wants the kids to have a room to come back to.

•

864. You need to know you can't change her moods, her fears, or her worries by yelling at her. Men have tried this for eons to no avail.

•

865. You need to know she doesn't find your burps or expulsions of gas hilarious.

866. You need to know she's not a
pyromaniac. She just likes candles.
Lots of them. Lit all at the same time.

•

867. You need to know she'll tell you that
you never say "I love you" though you
distinctly remember saying it
this morning. Doesn't matter.

•

868. You need to know she won't
find pouting manly.

•

869. You need to know she wishes you'd
make dinner every now and then. Even
barbecued elk. Something. Anything.

870. You need to know she doesn't really want to know about all your fears. Maybe she can handle your fear of plagues. Maybe your fear of the color red. But not too much more.

•

871. You need to know a candle can turn a dinner of Campbell's soup into a romantic evening.

•

872. You need to know she may interrupt your watching *24* to read you a paragraph from a book written two hundred years ago. While crying. Tell her you love it.

873. You need to know if she's
acting depressed, she won't just tell
you what's wrong. You'll have to ask.
Maybe more than ten times.

•

874. You need to know that, generally
speaking, women worry more than men do.
So there will be a lot of strange arguments
around the fact you're not worried enough.

•

875. You need to know vacuuming
the house can lead to even more fun
than giving her a massage.

•

876. You need to know she'd
really like you to shower.

877. You need to know to move all your exercise equipment to the garage even though it looks great in the bedroom. There's no alternative here.

•

878. You need to know that, although she likes the look of an unshaved guy, she doesn't want his face next to her skin. Yes, it's confusing.

•

879. You need to know to dress for dinner. You can't just show up in boxer shorts and think your presence will carry the day.

•

880. You need to know she'll think you're leaving her every morning. Even when you're just going to work.

881. You need to know to not get comfortable with her making more money than you do. According to *U.S. News & World Report*, wives generally aren't happy about this.

●

882. You need to know your wife could have three personalities in one day: full-time employee, working mom, and full-time wife.

●

883. You need to know it's her nature to beat a subject to death, pick it up, kill it again, then burn it, then gather all the ashes together, and beat it again. It's a gift only women have. You still have to listen.

Marriage and Menopause

884. You need to know menopause affects husbands *and* wives. No matter which one is going through it.

•

885. You need to know men go through a form of menopause too. True.

•

886. You need to know millions of couples have successfully navigated menopause without a divorce or a new Porsche.

•

887. You need to know menopause is a time when the sheets can get sweated up without anybody doing anything.

888. You need to know women tend be hot, cold, ecstatic, and suicidal all within a two-minute period. Men tend to remain confused.

•

889. You need to know a man in menopause is very much like a thirteen-year-old boy. Lost, dazed, and not sure what to do next.

•

890. You need to know that women in menopause tend to cry. Men tend to withdraw.

•

891. You need to know problems arise when both husband and wife hit menopause at the same time.

892. You need to know she could be dripping sweat while he's wearing his parka.

●

893. You need to know men feel helpless when their wives go through menopause. You can't stop the sweating, you can't stop the crying. The only thing you can stop is worrying about it.

●

894. You need to know that when a woman is suffering through menopause, men can't do anything right. Simply asking "How do you feel?" could launch World War III.

●

895. You need to know to tell each other how great they look in reading glasses.

896. You need to know it's best to not make any major decisions during this time. Not about your relationship or plastic surgery or getting a tattoo.

•

897. You need to know that getting into an argument with someone whose hormones are out of whack is a suicide mission.

•

898. You need to know this too shall pass. Sometime. Far, far out in the future. Maybe.

Dealing with a Man

899. You need to know that a woman thinks about her wedding all her life. He hasn't thought about it two minutes. He doesn't know what kind of flowers he wants. He doesn't care what the color theme should be.

●

900. You need to know men and women think about housework differently. For one thing, women think about it.

●

901. You need to know that if you want your husband to do something when you want him to do it, the way you want him to do it, chances are excellent he won't do anything.

902. You need to know he doesn't want
to talk about the marriage.
He wants to watch football.

•

903. You need to know that when he says,
"Nothing's wrong," nothing is wrong.
Certainly nothing's wrong enough
to interrupt football.

•

904. You need to know if you ask
him what he's thinking about,
it's either sex, food, or football.
That's why he doesn't want to tell you.

905. You need to know it's hard for a man to tell you what he's worried about. So start with something simple. Like, is he worried the team won't make the playoffs? Then work up.

•

906. You need to know men keep things. Like train sets. And baseball cards. And high school papers. This tendency may require you to find a bigger house.

•

907. You need to know you might spend a fortune on coloring and styling your hair, a manicure and pedicure, a facial and new make-up, and he still won't notice anything different.

908. You need to know it doesn't matter if you have a six-figure income. Your husband will always feel like he's supposed to be the primary breadwinner.

•

909. You need to know that when he's in the bathroom he doesn't want to have a conversation with you through the door. He will, however, happily talk to you on his cell.

•

910. You need to know men think soap, water, and maybe shampoo are all that's needed to get clean. He simply won't understand the importance of a loofah.

911. You need to know men listen differently from women. Women say "mm hmm" a lot when someone is talking to them. Men fiddle with the remote control.

912. You need to know that men tend to interrupt women. It's not just him. It's the entire breed.

913. You need to know he doesn't have ESP. Another male shortcoming.

914. You need to know men don't understand what "doing the laundry" means. Washing? Washing and drying? Washing, drying, and folding? And ironing? He doesn't know.

915. You need to know men are incapable of filling out forms.

•

916. You need to know a man feels loved when his wife respects him.

•

917. You need to know that when he's sick, he really wants you to stop everything and take care of him. Seriously. His mother would.

•

918. You need to know to not always quiz your husband about his feelings. What he's usually feeling is hungry.

•

919. You need to know men don't like to shave. He's not trying to make a fashion statement. He's avoiding razor burn.

920. You need to know he expects you to know what's wrong with the kids. You've read the books.

•

921. You need to know he thinks he's helping when he's telling you what to do.

•

922. You need to know he's always worried about you and the kids having enough. That's why it's hard for him to enjoy what he has without wanting more.

•

923. You need to know it bothers him when he thinks he doesn't have everything under control.

924. You need to know you won't understand his addiction to *Grand Theft Auto*. Love him through this.

•

925. You need to know if you want him to smell a certain way, you'll have to buy him cologne.

•

926. You need to know that he'll seem to disappear emotionally exactly when you really need him to confront a problem. Men want to think about the situation. They don't want to talk about it.

927. You need to know men take about
twenty or thirty minutes
to prepare themselves to talk
about a touchy issue. Don't make
a big deal out of it. Make dinner.

•

928. You need to know a man doesn't
like to cry in front of his wife.

•

929. You need to know he doesn't want to
think about shutters when it's fourth down
and the ball is on the two-yard line in
the final seconds of a tight game.

930. You need to know he'll drive you to the store to get tampons. But don't mention them, don't talk about them, and never, ever ask him to go inside and buy them.

•

931. You need to know that on car trips he wants to leave at the crack of dawn and get there in a hurry. Women want to have brunch and enjoy the drive.

•

932. You need to know you're going to have to show him what to do with an artichoke. And an eggplant.

•

933. You need to know he has no idea what he's thinking or feeling. So don't think you know.

934. You need to know that you carry the purse in the family. That's why he will stuff it with things he doesn't want to carry.

•

935. You need to know that the sound coming from downstairs early in the morning is him showing the kids how video games work.

•

936. You need to know that while he likes you with young-looking skin and makeup, he'll never fathom the cost.

•

937. You need to know you'll feed his friends stuff you wouldn't put in your mouth.

938. You need to know men don't
eat pimento cheese sandwiches.
Don't bother making them.

•

939. You need to know men
aren't genetically wired to appreciate
criticism. Instead of telling him
what he's doing wrong, make
a suggestion. Perfume helps too.

•

940. You need to know praise turns him on.

•

941. You need to know he likes to be
hugged even though he'd never tell you.

•

942. You need to know he has a fascination
for bodily noises. Don't ask why.

943. You need to know nagging
isn't sexy or effective.

•

944. You need to know he doesn't
need a mother. Even if he leaves
his underwear lying around.

•

945. You need to know he's counting on
you to not finish your dinner. So he can.
Assuming it's not pimento cheese.

•

946. You need to know he really
doesn't know how to change a diaper.
He never played with dolls.

•

947. You need to know men aren't into
"sharing the moment." They're worrying
about paying the mortgage next month.

948. You need to know all men need tools.
An electric drill. A chain saw. A 2000 piece
tool set. He may never use them. But he
needs to know they're in the garage.

•

949. You need to know he'll never
feel he's making enough money.

•

950. You need to know if you make
more money than he does, his ego may
not recover. Men are weird that way.

•

951. You need to know eating off your plate
uninvited is his way of saying he trusts you.

952. You need to know you could be married to him for fifty years and still not know he's always hated *Grey's Anatomy*.

•

953. You need to know he ranks golf right below food, clothing, and shelter. Arguing with him about this will just make him want to go to the driving range.

•

954. You need to know he will be furious if your cell phone is turned off or uncharged. Just a hint.

•

955. You need to know that unless he does the shopping—for food, diapers, and medicine—he'll never know how much things cost.

956. You need to know he views the bathroom the way you might view a library. It's a place to get serious reading done.

•

957. You need to know the reason he hasn't picked up his shoes is because he's lost them.

•

958. You need to know he doesn't think a pile of laundry is that important. Yelling at him will just make him think your hormones are acting up.

•

959. You need to know that most men can live with dirty clothes piled to the ceiling until he runs out of underwear. That's when he'll think about washing them.

960. You need to know men lose things.
Cell phones. Wallets. Keys. Sometimes
their cars. Criticizing won't help.

•

961. You need to know most men
aren't good at communicating
or expressing their feelings.

•

962. You need to know he sees the bed
as a place for sleep and sex. You see it
as a piece of furniture that requires
accessories and constant attention.

•

963. You need to know he really and truly
has no earthly idea what to do with
Tupperware. And he doesn't understand
the big deal about losing a lid.

964. You need to know if you come to him with a problem, he will tell you how to solve it, then get back to watching TV. He will think his work is done.

●

965. You need to know he'll remember something you said about his hair two years ago, but he will forget you asked him to go to the store this morning.

●

966. You need to know he thinks your car is the mom car and the stuff in the backseat could be contagious.

967. You need to know your husband will understand the value of maids after both of you spend all Saturday cleaning, vacuuming, picking up, dusting, washing, ironing, and folding.

•

968. You need to know he will confuse your emotional need for affection with a desire to hop into bed. It's in his DNA.

•

969. You need to know he can let you hold the remote control for only about an hour. Once a month. Watch for hyperventilation.

•

970. You need to know if you come home after spending $200 at the hairdresser, your hair should look like it. Subtlety doesn't work on men.

971. You need to know that, by their nature, men don't want to talk about their plans and dreams because things could go awry. Find other ways to get him talking.

•

972. You need to know he doesn't love his friends more than he loves you. He just knows they don't want any chores done, they don't expect him to make a living, and they all want to watch the game.

•

973. You need to know that even if you have evidence that his best friend's wife is a screaming, narcissistic, selfish fraud, you're not to share this with your husband. Don't mess with the male bonding.

974. You need to know he'll want to store his bicycle in the living room because he thinks it too hot for it in the garage.

•

975. You need to know that men have a thing for T-shirts. They'll keep thirty of them and wear about three. There's safety in numbers.

•

976. You need to know that if you're taking a car trip, he will try to use his innate sense of direction instead of a map.

•

977. You need to know he'll think he's done something significant when he changes a light bulb or cleans the garage. Don't miss this opportunity to praise him.

978. You need to know that, while he shares your enthusiasm for decorating, he thinks the money could better be spent on a big screen.

•

979. You need to know he likes letting you win. He doesn't like you beating him.

•

980. You need to know men don't like "process and share." They want to solve your problem and then go back to the football game. And that's what they do with their own problems, too.

981. You need to know the whole picnic thing mystifies him. He doesn't like eating on blankets, he doesn't like ants, and he doesn't like getting hot now that air conditioning has been invented.

•

982. You need to know he would rather stick needles in his eye than go shopping.

•

983. You need to know that when he asks, "How was your day?" he wants a brief recap. Not a blow-by-blow, minute-by-minute reliving of the last twelve hours.

984. You need to know that, genetically, he can live on barbecue alone.

•

985. You need to know that because you went with him to seedy country-and-western bars fifteen years ago, he thinks you still like them. Really.

•

986. You need to know he doesn't like antique hunting. He likes TV hunting.

•

987. You need to know he'd rather not go to the monster truck pull with you if all you're going to do is whine and demand to leave in thirty minutes. Tell him to go with his friends.

988. You need to know men worry about money when they're on vacation. It helps them relax.

•

989. You need to know that men think doing repairs and yard work on Saturday equals a woman doing the laundry, cleaning, shopping, cooking, and picking things up all week long.

Marriage and
the Best Years

990. You need to know that, over
the years, happiness creeps up on you.
You realize one day that you're eighty
years old and still madly in love with him.
Though he's a wacko on football.

•

991. You need to know that
research shows martial satisfaction
rises when the kids hit the road.

•

992. You need to know many
long-time married couples are wildly
incompatible. They just agree to
love each other, differences and all.

993. You need to know that, after spending twenty-five or thirty years continually needing a bigger home, a smaller one now has a lot of appeal. Of course, you'll need to remodel it.

•

994. You need to know there is life after soccer practice, football games, proms, and college entrance exams. Like pets.

•

995. You need to know you'll be tempted to ruin a professionally decorated living room with two La-Z-Boys.

•

996. You need to know you can now shop at all the places you couldn't afford when you had college tuition payments.

997. You need to know
the kids need to know when
your monetary support will end.

•

998. You need to know to keep
making passes at each other.

•

999. You need to know that even though
you talk about moving to the mountains or
the beach, you'll live where your kids live.

1000. You need to know that, after years
of raising kids, paying off loans, dealing
with health issues, and learning
to live with each other, you'll find bliss.

•

1001. You need to know to thank
God for making it all possible.

*Other books in the 1001 THINGS Series
by Harry Harrison*

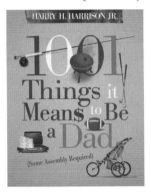

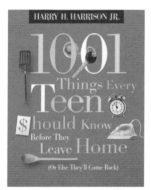

HARRY H. HARRISON JR.

1001
Things Every
TEEN
$hould Know
Before They
Leave Home

(Or Else They'll Come Back)

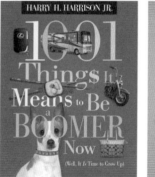

HARRY H. HARRISON JR.

1001
Things It
Means to Be
a
BOOMER
Now

(Well, It Is Time to Grow Up)

HARRY H. HARRISON JR.

1001
Things Every
College
Student
Needs to Know

(Like Buying Your Books before Exams Start)